Galloping Geese on the Rio Grande Southern

Tin Feathers and Gasoline Fumes

by Stanley Rhine

Reprinted from the
Colorado Rail Annual
No. 9 - 1971

MANAGING EDITOR
Cornelius W. Hauck
ASSOCIATE EDITOR
Gordon Chappell
CONSULTING EDITOR
Robert W. Richardson
PUBLISHED AND DISTRIBUTED BY
the Colorado Railroad Museum

The Colorado Railroad Museum is operated by the **Colorado Railroad Historical Foundation, Inc.,** a non-profit Colorado educational institution. Your membership in and support for the Foundation are earnestly solicited. Dues begin at $10 per year for Active Membership.

BOX 10, GOLDEN CO 80402

VISIT THE MUSEUM, OPEN DAILY YEAR 'ROUND

ISBN 0-918654-40-8

Printed and bound in the United States of America

the full story of the unique
Galloping Geese motor cars
of the Rio Grande Southern narrow gauge

A trio of Geese preserved at the Colorado Railroad Museum (R. C. Hill)

Galloping Goose Country *R. W. Richardson*

Ruminations on the Origin and Evolution of the Galloping Goose

Tin Feathers and Gasoline Fumes

Stan Rhine

Even 20 years after the fact, it would appear that Lucius Beebe's *Mixed Train Daily* observation that the Rio Grande Southern Railroad was ". . . one of the most completely remarkable railroads of the world" is still ". . . only to indulge an advised and considered generality." It was remarkable in its conception and in its invention of the famous Galloping Goose, and it remained remarkable through the turning of the last wheel and the pulling of the last spike.

Its traces are still remarkable.

Of the monuments of this railroad, few are more awe-inspiring than the gangling trestle at Ames. That structure is impressive when viewed from the highway (Colorado 145), where one sees its spindly flanks gleaming silver-grey against a vertical expanse of mountain that shames the puny efforts of man beneath. It is impressive when viewed from the dirt road past Vance Junction and Ilium, flitting behind the trees, an evanescent framework among the arboreal greenness. It is impressive when viewed from the edge of the abyss which it spans, its tieless timbers grinning vacantly like a broken skull.

It is peaceful now at Ames trestle. The songs of the birds are no longer interrupted by the bellow of a locomotive, the cascade of cinders, the screams of flanges, and the cacophony of a Goose. Ames tank still stands. There is an occasional tie, almost merged with its resting place. Vance Junction is the ghostliest of ghost towns, strewn with the debris of 60 years of improbability. The railroad has become almost as intangible as the shattered hopes and dreams of its builders and operators. Yet there are still sufficient traces to jog the memory of those who have experienced it, and arouse the curiosity of those who have not.

The RGS has rolled its last dice with destiny—and lost. That much of it still survives is a mixture of luck and chance. But besides the slowly eroding traces of its being, it has left other, more tangible reminders that it was not something that Lucius Beebe and Charles Clegg made up late one soggy night aboard the "Virginia City." There are a number of cars and locomotives scattered across the countryside, in varying states of semi-preservation or disrepair. In some ways this equipment is no less remarkable than the railroad. A

In the early days of the century, before paved highways reached into the San Juans, the Rio Grande Southern's rails were burnished daily by such quaint varnish hauls as these. At the top, RGS 10 (one of the Road's original second-hand 2-8-0's) blasts up the west side of Dallas Divide with the Telluride passenger. Center, first No. 23 (a light, ex-D&RGW Baldwin tenwheeler) leans into a curve with the Durango passenger train near Dix, east of Mancos, about 1907. At bottom, RGS first 25 poses at the Durango platform with a similar consist during the same period. This sturdy Rome tenwheeler, obtained from the Rio Grande Western, had begun life on the Denver Circle Railroad. (Bottom, Lad Arend Coll.; others, Museum Collection.)

rough count shows that the company at one time or another owned about 1,200 cars and 46 steam locomotives, a string which, if it could be assembled, would reach from Vance Junction up across Ames trestle, over recently razed Butterfly trestle, through Ophir to Matterhorn, just downgrade from Trout Lake. But owing to the poor condition of the cars (one large batch from the D&RG-RGW before the turn of the century and another from the Colorado and Southern in 1938) the RGS was a perambulating junkyard — if, in fact, the cars were even in good enough condition to be moved. For example, although all of the stock cars bought by the RGS from the Colorado and Southern (45) were operated, at least for a short time, only 44 of the 80 box cars were apparently ever operated at all.

The Ridgway yards were a delight to the eyes of the collector of the bizarre, but a curse to the operating department. Letters from officials at Ridgway complained first to the D&RG and finally to the receiver in Denver about the "junk" clogging the tracks outside, and pleaded for relief. Eventually most of the early cars were scrapped where they stood, and some 60 ex-Colorado and Southern cars left the property. Judging by telegrams received at Ridgway from Gunnison, noting the absence of uncoupling levers, brakewheels and brake rods from the departing cars, those the RGS kept must have been the best of them.

Among the remarkable equipment was that used for maintenance of way. Many of these cars were left over from the first housecleaning of the Ridgway yards in the waning 1890's. So singular were some of the alterations, and so strange was the appearance of these "M-of-W" oddities that they deserve extensive treatment by themselves. No less singular were the cars which became a first class Colorado institution, the Galloping Geese. They came about because of a sequence of events which probably could not have happened any place else.

★ ★ ★

The history of the RGS is but a flash in the time of man, but in the ways of man, it is sufficiently complicated that any reasonable chronicle would require book length treatment. Suffice it to say that the RGS never lived up to the fond hopes of Mears and his backers as an ambulatory gold mine. The 162.6 mile Rio Grande Southern Railroad was not built as a "shortcut" to cover the 12 precipitous miles remaining between the ends of the rails at Red Mountain and Ouray. It was spiked down to serve the rich mining operations at the rich town itself, Rico, and at Telluride and Ophir. In 1890, work had begun toward the mining camps of the mountains remote from the twin railheads of Ridgeway and Durango. Reaching only part way to the destination of Rico by the first winter, the rails nonetheless were kept shiny by the busy wheels of a multitude of profitable narrow gauge trains shuttling back and forth. In the fall of the following year, track had been pushed into Rico from the north and crews tied the final knot somewhere south of Rico before the year 1891 finished its business and tramped reluctantly off into the gathering snow.

The railroad succeeded in tucking a tidy sum under its mattress in 1892, and the future looked rosy. But in the very next year, Congress repealed the Sherman Silver Purchase act. The mines, no longer profitable, produced little but echoes and the towns sank into a fitful sleep. Passenger business thrived temporarily, as thousands swarmed to the closely-spaced rails of the RGS—bound for anywhere. Money evaporated, and only a slight precipitate of the formerly booming business was left. The mountains closed in upon the lonely little railroad, whose reason for existence had disappeared as quickly as the railroad was built. Hence, the great depression found the RGS long since depressed. The Ames slide of 1929 had severed the line, and it was estimated that some $30,000 would be required to restore operation. In December of that year, the court appointed Victor A. Miller as receiver, and charged him with maintaining the steel artery of the San Juan mountains.

The task facing Miller was formidable. He had to restore operation in the face of these physical difficulties, and a series of other problems which the bankrupt road faced. There was no money in the treasury. There were but few serviceable locomotives and cars. Taxes were long overdue, and the track and facilities had been badly neglected. Nevertheless, Miller resumed operation. On the first day of June of 1930, crews attacked the Ames slide with borrowed equipment. Shoving aside the tender growth of spring, they burrowed through nearly 200 feet of material, reportedly 50 feet deep in places. Within a month, they had sutured the San Juans back together, and at a cost of less than $2,000.

Miller instituted the policy of using the RGS's own engines rather than renting locomotives from the D&RGW. He also began insisting that the company repair its engines rather than sending them to Alamosa for repairs at inflated prices. He hired Forest White as General Manager at a salary of $5,000.00 a year, and terminated D&RGW supervision, thereby saving $15,000.00 per year. He renegotiated the terminal contract at Durango, saving $7,000.00 a year. The savings in locomotive rental amounted to $10,000.00 and repairs to $25,000.00 per year. Thus, in a very short time, Miller had managed not to spend some $57,000.00 per year: an impressive, if largely paper, savings. Having made this much progress, he began looking for other ways to save.

In order to effect further economies, he had to find some way to reduce the cost of train operation. There were a limited number of possibilities. The number of trains being operated could be reduced, the frequency of operation could be reduced, maintenance of equipment and track could be reduced, or less expensive substitute service could be inaugurated. There was yet another possibility: operation could be terminated. This would be a drastic solution—some would say no solution at all—and a final one. Fortunately Miller did not elect to take the "easy way" out.

The RGS had been in the railroad business for nearly 40 years, and the habit hung on . . . they wanted to make money, but they wanted to do it by staying in the railroad business, an impression not always projected by modern conglomerate railroad-and-everything-else corporations. Early in 1931, they began to seriously investigate the feasibility of substitute service. Why they adopted the particular solution for which they became justly famous is not at all apparent from the records, but fandom has agreed that it was an inspired choice—inspired by poverty it is true, but inspired nonetheless.

★ ★ ★

There appear to be no detailed accounts which reflect the state of mind in this period of searching for a solution. However, contemporary Colorado & Southern files show some interesting studies which they were conducting. They were also investigating possible substitutes for steam trains to be used on their narrow gauge branch from Denver to Leadville. They considered a variety of proposals; the purchase of new equipment, such as bizarre machines articulated in two or three places, which looked rather like a grade-crossing accident between an amputated coach, a milk truck and a horse trailer. They also considered major remodeling of available equipment, including the powering of coaches with gasoline engines. The C&S finally opted for the easy alternative, and gave up the ghost. Had they followed the lead of the RGS, perhaps the third rail would not have been removed from the Denver station.

What both the RGS and the C&S sought was a self-propelled unit which could be operated with a minimal crew, and would have accommodations for both package freight (LCL) and the hardy few passengers who would brave the combination of mountain railroading and narrow gauge track. This vehicle would have to operate dependably in all kinds of weather, some of it downright cold, and through ice and snow. It would have to at least maintain existing schedules, and be fairly inexpensive to operate. Above all, it must not be expensive to build or maintain.

The 1965 ANNUAL carried pictures of a Model T Ford built and owned by a garageman at Como. He used to go for weekend spins on the Colorado and Southern, and took railfan Bruce Triplett along one Sunday. By pulling a pin in the steering gear and wrenching the steering wheel, the Ford could be made to crawl off the track and waddle into town for gas. Triplett recalls an enjoyable time, opening fences and jouncing along.

The Denver and Rio Grande had four—all different makes and models. They sometimes sent these inspection cars teetering over the system in convoy. The Rio Grande Southern had also converted a Model T Ford to operate on narrow gauge track, but likely aroused the ire of Henry Ford by their great alterations. About the only thing that Ford himself would have recognized were the huge acetylene headlights and the hood. The rest of it was a somewhat unesthetic mix of handcar wheels and uncomfortable-looking seats.

This four-wheeler was built in 1913, and wrecked rather spectacularly in 1925. Correspondence suggested that since about $250.00 would be required to rectify the damages, the Rio Grande Southern could get along without this breezy machine, Motor Number 1. There would be a gap of a half dozen years before there would be another Motor Number 1, the first of the famous Galloping Geese. Although there appears to be some confusion on this point, the Ford inspection car, Motor Number 1, and the first Goose, Motor Number 1, were obviously not the same. The second number 1 was much bigger than the first number 1, but it was still more of a gosling than a Goose.

Although a fair amount of imagination was also incorporated, Goose No. 1 was more Buick than anything else. It possessed the hood and front portion of a Buick body and a flat bed on which a stake truck body had been built. Superintendent Forest White on May 11, 1931, described this machine as having a closed cab with a seat running the entire width and an open stake body. It was hardly what one would have been tempted to call "rakish." This marvel of advanced engineering was carried on a single pair of wooden spoked wheels at the rear and a swiveling four-wheeled truck at the front. All of the parts that were used

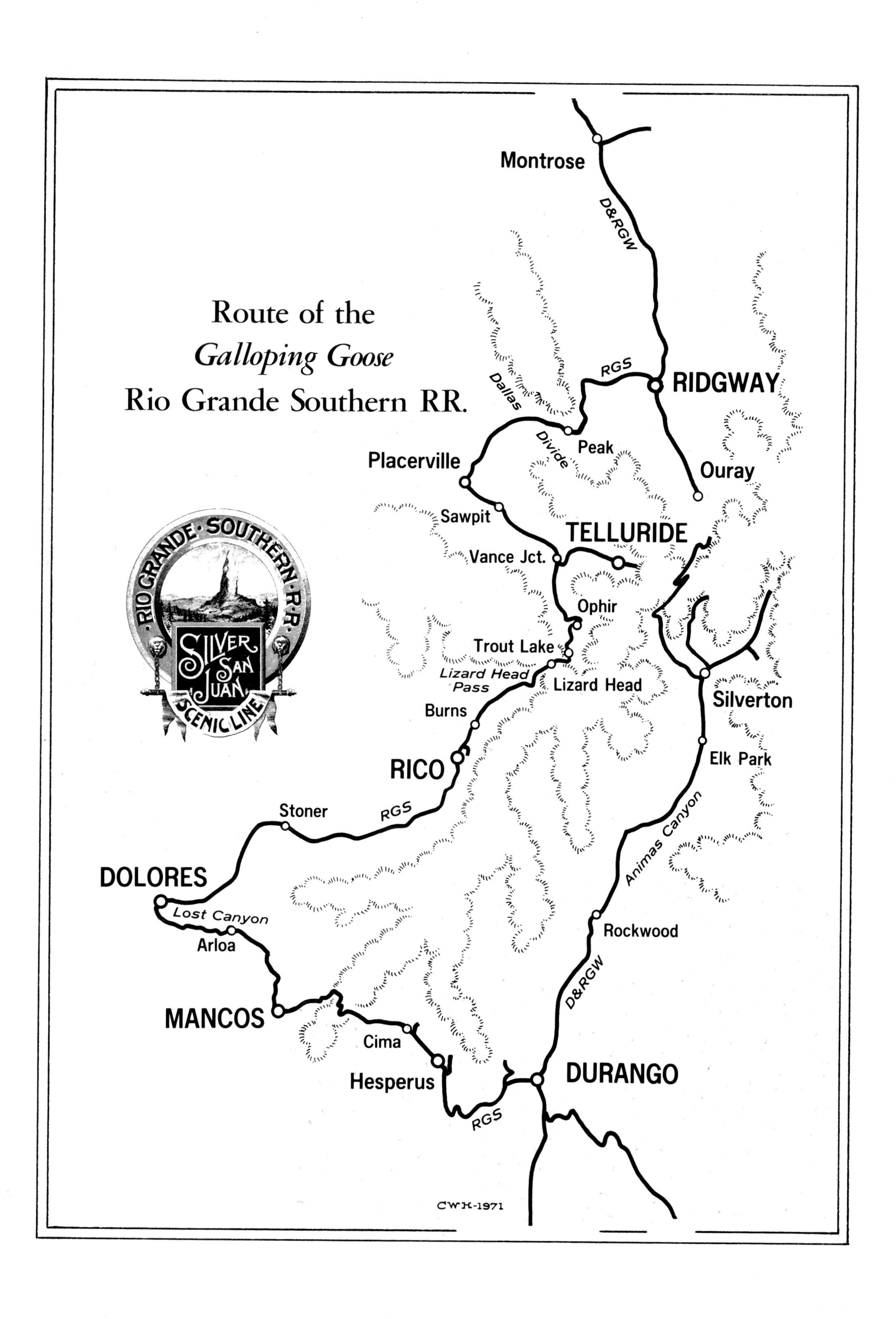

Route of the
Galloping Goose
Rio Grande Southern RR.
Montrose
D&RGW
RGS
RIDGWAY
Dallas
Divide
Peak
Ouray
Placerville
Sawpit
TELLURIDE
Vance Jct.
Ophir
Trout Lake
Lizard Head
Pass
Lizard Head
Burns
RICO
Silverton
Elk Park
Stoner
RGS
Animas Canyon
DOLORES
Lost Canyon
Arloa
Rockwood
D&RGW
MANCOS
Cima
Hesperus
DURANGO
RGS
RIO GRANDE · SOUTHERN · R.R.
SILVER SAN JUAN
SCENIC LINE
CWH-1971

When the Rio Grande Southern's pioneer Galloping Goose No. 1 was completed, it was rolled out in front of the roundhouse in its shiny new paint and photographed for the Company's files—and for posterity. In fact, these official photos are the only photos of No. 1 known to exist; if nothing else they reveal the utter simplicity and unpretentiousness of the design and construction of this first Goose. (Stanley D. Schwedler Collection.) No. 1 served the RGS for only a relatively short time—it was soon supplanted by the larger and more commodious Pierce-Arrow Geese — and its ultimate fate is unknown. Probably it was used for a time for a source of parts for nos. 2 and 6. In any event, photographs of No. 1 are understandably rare.

That the RGS Geese could trace their ancestry back to the Rio Grande Southern and D&RGW Model-T Ford inspection cars in only the most limited fashion can be seen from examining the photo at right, of D&RGW car M-3 at Durango in 1924 (R. H. Kindig Coll.). Goose No. 2, first example of the orthodox style, marked an even greater departure from the inspection-car pattern than had No. 1. In its first version (bottom), it revealed a basis as a four-door Buick; once again, the photograph is an official company view, and more candid views are lacking (Museum Coll.). Subsequently No. 2 was rebuilt with Pierce-Arrow components, as shown at right at Durango in 1940 (Richard H. Kindig), and it is this latter version that is preserved today at the Colorado Railroad Museum.

Numbers 3 and 4 were the first of the "big" Geese, and when No. 4 was completed in the spring of 1932 the RGS wheeled it out onto the line for a test run and official company-file photographs. Above it is posed at the wye on Dallas Divide (Mike Decker Coll.), while below it nestles gingerly on one of the Railroad's numerous trestles (Museum Coll.). Evident in these photos is its Pierce-Arrow limousine origin (No. 3, for instance, was bought from Kumpf Motor Company in Denver for $400) and the dark, high-gloss auto enamel finish.

came to just under $300.00, and the total cost was a mere $828.55.

In preparation for fielding their first Goose, the RGS also precipitously purchased an ailing model 6-40 1915 Hudson from A. J. Croonenbergs for $300.00. When a careful inspection showed it to be perilously close to expiring, it was quickly sold to another local resident: an unnamed and unfortunate individual—not the first nor the last to be surprised by their dealings with the RGS.

Assistant to the receiver, F. C. Krauser, objected to the open body of number 1. No wonder! The RGS had received a painfully detailed letter from the regional headquarters of the Post Office Department in Omaha, citing late arrivals in Telluride (as much as six hours on separate occasions), and complained from dissatisfied passengers, if there were more than one or two, of the need to sit on the mail bags in the open stake body.

The Post Office Department claimed that reports had it that the "motormen" could not see behind the body, and that there was a danger of the mail being pilfered. The Southern calmly replied that there was an ample window (about 12 inches x 16 inches) through which the driver could survey the receding track and the mails as well.

Nevertheless, they acted upon the complaint. On July 21, 1931 White noted that the marvelous number 1 could accommodate seven passengers, and that the open bed could be covered with a canvas tied at the sides and end to secure the mail. Less than a month later, White sketched the layout of number 1 for the Post Office people. That sketch shows a five passenger seat behind the motorman's seat. That estimate of passenger capacity would appear to be generous, as the sketch also shows the width as six feet, six inches, which would allow each of the five passengers a chummy fifteen and one-half inches of sitting space, a space that would better accommodate the Stanley Laurels than the Oliver Hardys of Southwestern Colorado.

White said that the sides were solid, that there was a four feet, five inch, door at the rear of the mail compartment, that the roof was sheet iron, and that ". . . ceiling (was) used for sides and ends." By "ceiling" he presumably meant "beaded ceiling," a novelty wood paneling used in old farmhouses, railroad stations, cabooses and passenger cars. A solid board partition had been placed between the passengers and the 6 foot, 9 inch-long, mail compartment. This description suggested that within two months from the time that number 1 had been placed in service, the RGS had received a complaint from the Post Office Department and had quickly moved to modify number 1 to conform to the requirements of a closed and locked mail compartment, by building a wooden shed about the size of a squat two-holer behind the chopped-off Buick body.

Although pictures of number 1 in its original state have been unearthed, none show it after the road modified it as described above. Given the RGS's contented purring over its first Goose, it would be strange indeed had it left no further impression upon emulsion. That does not mean that the road encountered no further problems. Since they had attempted something rather more daring than the usual replace-the-wheels-with-flanged-ones found on so many other roads, and because of additional complications resulting from squeezing it down to narrow gauge, problems erupted. A report of July 8, 1931 showed both axles broken. Presumably they meant that both axles on the front truck were fractured. Slightly later, they also apparently broke the rear wheels, and had trouble replacing them.

White chided the Western Auto Wrecking Company of Grand Junction for delaying a shipment of replacement hubs for number 1 on October 6, 1931 by putting them on the D&RGW train rather than the D&RGW bus, which arrived some hours earlier. He reminded them that the RGS was operating a railroad and that they could not be delayed by the necessity of waiting for their parts to arrive on that slow narrow gauge train. He then instructed them to call collect if they were unable to make the bus connection in the future. As a frustrating aside, a hurried trip had to be made to Montrose for the parts, and when the parts finally arrived from Grand Junction, they proved to be the wrong kind.

Obviously the running of a railroad had its disappointments. But the savings resulting in the operation of the new machine was not one of them. After trial service in 1931, White estimated to Auditor C. W. Graebing that $462.19 had been saved by running Motor number 1 instead of a steam train between Telluride and Dolores for half of the month of June. At that rate, the motor would have paid back the original cost of construction in slightly less than a month! It was clear that this little rolling gold mine was the wave of the future. This was indeed the Goose that laid the golden egg. The Southern determined at once to build more motors—but this time, they would have passenger comfort and would do something to keep the Omaha Post Office headquarters from writing them so many nasty letters.

★ ★ ★

On June 10, 1931, O. H. Steinman, Trainmaster, sent out Bulletin number 14, which said that ef-

No. 5 was constructed from a slightly newer Pierce-Arrow (1928 model 36) and is shown here in its pre-war styling, in a number of poses. Above, Dick Kindig found it at Lizard Head in 1942. At left, it gets a needed drink of water (above), and poses (below) with one of its better-known jockeys Jim Cooper, next to one of the line's tall trestles (both, Lad Arend Coll.). Below, it makes a brief stop at MP 11 on Dallas Divide. back in 1940 (Guy Dunscomb Coll.).

fective June 16, trains #375-376, Durango-Dolores would be Goosed. Applications were being taken for "motormen" at $165.00 per month, with no overtime. At this time number 1 was in use between Telluride and Dolores. Work on number 2 was progressing, but not as rapidly as they had hoped. After all, number 2 was a far more elaborate vehicle than number 1. By July 8, 1931, Jack Odenbaugh had cut down the Buick body (the back of the body had been chopped off square), and had worked on the front truck.

Soon after the maiden voyage of no. 1, and a month before the completion of no. 2, the earliest official Goose schedule came into effect, dated July 1, 1931. Departing a D&RGW connection at Ridgeway, a steam train rolled south to Telluride, arriving there at 9:10 p.m. The next morning, it departed Telluride at 10:05 a.m., and arrived in Dolores at 1:50 p.m. Some 25 minutes were allowed for the transfer of passengers and mail to the idling bird, which departed in a cloud of exhaust fumes at 2:15 p.m. It fluttered into Durango at 5:08 p.m., just in time to pick up passengers deposited on the platform by the recently-arrived *San Juan.* Its departure was scheduled for 5:10 p.m., leaving a leisurely two minutes in which to shove the Durango-bound passengers out, the Dolores-bound ones in, and to accomplish a transfer of mail and express.

Racing the setting sun westward to Dolores (and losing), no. 1 staggered into the station at 8:15 p.m., and heaved a sigh of relief as its ignition key was turned off. Thus, the unsuspecting Ridgway-destined traveler who had so lately enjoyed the relative oppulence of the *San Juan's* parlor car suffered the indignity of being stuffed into the cramped number 1, and was unceremoniously dumped, reeking of tobacco juice and gasoline, into the dusty streets of the gem of Dolores County. To make matters worse, he would be obliged to enjoy its hospitality until the following San Juan sunrise tinted the distant peaks with the first delicate shades of dawn, and the Ridgway train eased out of town to the deafening crash of couplers, and the groans of late risers at 5:45 a.m. Hemmed in by the surrounding hills, Dolores was constantly reminded of the presence of the railroad, which even with the infrequency of its comings and goings, must have made as much impression on the collective consciousness as did the Santa Fe in Albuquerque.

Goose number 2, now residing at the Colorado Railroad Museum, was a considerable step forward in design from number 1. Where number 1 had had only a swiveling front truck, number 2 was mounted on two swiveling trucks. As it would turn out, the swivel plates did not conform to ICC regulations and had to be rebuilt some years later, but this machine represented a daring step forward in complexity and serviceability. Number 1 was weighed in at 5,300 pounds on February 22, 1932, after almost a year in service. By comparison, the completed number 2 weighed 10,300 pounds—almost double the weight of Motor number 1.

It was an immediate hit. The larger machine was a Buick "master six" 4 door sedan spliced to a long rear frame which carried a 16 foot mail and express compartment, provided with large lockable doors. It seemed to have satisfied the Post Office Department in all respects, except perhaps for an occasional lapse into late arrival, a circumstance created in part by the undulating terrain and the heavy snows. In response to a request for explanation for delays, White wrote Krauser, ". . . I believe that all things considered our motors have done remarkably well. We have always gotten through, which is more than the D&RGW have been able to do and I do not believe there is such an awful difference in the snow on our two lines." But number 2 was not the epitome of trouble-free operation. After only two years of operation, the RGS tried to pawn it off on one of the rarest of human beings—a potential customer.

On December 15, 1931, J. Ferguson wrote Ed Randow that he had been trying for a week to find out why number 2 should gulp 32 gallons of gas for a round trip. He had made numerous adjustments to the engine and had finally loosened the brakes, and hoped that one of these measures, or the combination, would rectify the problem. Apparently it did, since there is nothing further in the files, though loosening of the brakes would seem to be a risky solution.

On September 17, 1931, motormen were advised to stop allowing non-revenue passengers to crowd revenue passengers out of the "choice seats." One wonders which ones they were . . . number 1 had been designed for 1 or 2 passengers in addition to the driver, and number 2 could accommodate 3 or 4 passengers with as much comfort as a Goose could generate. Extra passengers could be allowed to sit on top of the cab, or in back with the mail. Considering the complaints of the Post Office Department, this latter seating arrangement was probably discouraged. Passengers were thus reduced to siting on each others laps, on the roof, or on the pilot. It would be most interesting to discover by which means overflow passengers were accommodated in the two smallest railcars.

It appeared that something of even greater passenger and express capacity would have to be devised. The RGS had apparently anticipated this

Bill Pennington rode the line in 1940 and photographed Goose No. 5 in locations that were to become familiar to many railfans — right, at Placerville depot, and below, by the depot at Vance Junction. The old coach-section house was a remnant of the RGS' plusher days. (Guy Dunscomb Coll.).

demand, and number 3, the first large Goose, was completed only 4 months after number 2. Company records do not indicate how much time was required to hatch a Galloping Goose, although the construction of number 5 from initial parts hunting to regular service seems to have been accomplished in a mere 3 months.

Goose building seems to have been cut and fit. There were no blueprints, a fact for which the road apologized when responding to requests for information from other railroads. Number 1 was completed in June of 1931, and two months were torn off the shop calendar before number 2 was added to the roster. Four additional months were required for the fabrication of the first large Goose which was completed in December. The denizens of Detroit could well be envious at the rapid modification and perfection of the Galloping Geese. In only 6 months from the completion of the first little railcar, the comparatively large "standard" Goose had evolved.

This evolution can be illustrated by a comparison of the gross weights of the first 3 machines constructed. Number 1 weighed 5,300 pounds, number 2 weighed 10,300, and number 3 weighed 14,800 pounds. The 7 foot mail compartment of number 1 evolved into a 16 foot express compartment on number 2, and a 24 foot express body on number 3. Passenger capacity increased from about 4 or 5 in number 1 and 2 to 10 in number 3 and subsequent Geese. The horsepower leaped from 28 plus (A.L.A.M. rating, not brake horsepower) in numbers 1 and 2 to 39 plus in number 3 and following cars. Overall length went from less than 20 feet for number 1 to 29 feet, 11 inches, for number 2, and 43 feet, 3 inches, for number 3 and similar dimensions for following machines.

Although number 3 became the "standard" of this very non-standard railroad, subsequent hatchings provided subtle variations on the theme, which can be pondered by the Goose fancier. Mechanically, the 3 and 4 were mostly Pierce-Arrow model "33" limousines, and were as identical as the sporadic availability of used cars and the craftsmanship of Jack Odenbaugh, the "Mother Goose" of Ridgway, could make them. Number 5 began its life as a slightly later (1927-28) model "36" sedan, while number 7 was again the model "33". The specifications of all of these machines were similar, but the 7 varied from the others in that it was provided with an express compartment 2 feet longer, and with air brakes.

The large Goose was truly a remarkable machine. Victor Miller's description sounds as if it might have been written as he was attempting recovery from a late-night romp with chocolate bar and dill pickle sandwiches, chased down with mince pie and over-the-hill apple cider. However, that description was not the work of an affected mind, but rather an account of reality. Had the RGS been able to go out and buy something "off-the-shelf", or had they had money to build with all new equipment, they would not have been likely to have produced such a nightmare of a machine. But financial circumstance forced this solution: a nightmare that was a different kind of horse altogether. It worked, and it worked so well that the RGS held together a few more years because of it.

Miller said that a Pierce-Arrow ". . . model 33 of the year 1926, is spread in the body to the ordinary width of a narrow gauge car . . . the chassis remodeled to fit two four-wheel trucks . . . a light metal trailer running on a third narrow gauge four-wheel truck, is permanently affixed to the rear of the automobile . . ." Otto Mears, who was accused of building his mountain toll roads and railroads so crooked that a jackass required a hinge in the middle to negotiate curves, would have been pleased with the articulated Geese. The remodeled Pierce-Arrow body and the boxy 2 inch x 2 inch wooden-framed express body shared the center truck, from which they lurched in their own separate rates and directions. Why did the Goose gallop? Partly because of this structure and partly because of the irregular track. Prospective passengers have been known to consider revising their intent to penetrate the mountain fastness upon seeing this apparition slide into the depot, everything going in different directions like a noisy bowlful of silver Jello.

Work Goose number 6 was quite another matter. Like the 1 and 2, it was not articulated, and rested its 25 foot length upon but two trucks. The flat bed body was provided with low stake sides. Although it was built with a Buick "master six" body like the 1 and 2 (and may even have used the body and other parts from the then-recently deceased number 1), later pictures show it with a Pierce-Arrow body of about the same vintage as the 5. It was used for inspection, maintenance, and even as a helper.

But, there is a problem . . . what could you honestly call a cross between an automobile and a box car? The Southern began by calling them "motors", as distinguished from "motor car", the gandy dancer's friend. Nonetheless, they sometimes slipped up, and called them "motor car", a confusing business to say the least. The 1933 y-clept, "Automobile Train", bestowed by the *Express Messenger* Magazine, is descriptive enough, but a trifle strung out for anyone wanting a quick

Early in May, 1942, Guy Dunscomb made a trip over the RGS in Goose No. 4 that produced the memorable photo at right. The scene is Hagens, 5 miles out of Ridgway, and No. 4 has backed into the passing siding (cluttered with box cars) to let inbound Goose No. 3 clatter by on the last leg of its run to Ridgway. It may be springtime in the lower reaches of the Rockies, but the Uncompahgres in the background are still laced with snow. By the time No. 4 reached the 10,000-foot heights of Lizard Head Pass (below) it had picked up patches of snow on its pilot plow, and the towering peaks of the San Juans surrounding the little log depot and snow-sheds looked forbiddingly bleak and wintry. A ride over the RGS under such circumstances, in the relative warmth of spring, would convince any skeptic that operating the RGS year-round was not all "fun and games". (Both photos, Guy Dunscomb.)

After leaving Dolores late that afternoon, No. 4 had its second meet of the day at Smalley, in Lost Canyon, where they were forced to wait in isolated idleness for 45 minutes. *(Guy Dunscomb.)*

When the Goose met the D&RGW San Juan at Durango, there was always a certain amount of mail, LCL and express to transfer. On the stormy July afternoon in 1941 when Bob Richardson was waiting for the No. 3 to leave town (above), the whole crew had pitched in to get the job done before the heavens opened up and all concerned would be drenched. (R. W. Richardson.) During the Miller administration the RGS maintained a terminal just west of Durango, and in 1940 Gerry Best found the No. 3 nesting in a shed there (below); a long string of old RGS locomotives stood derelict in the background. (G. M. Best.) No. 3 found the going more difficult one winter day back in the late thirties (at left) and had to get help from one of the line's steamers. (R. H. Kindig Coll.).

No 4 still presented something approaching its original appearance back in 1940, when it was snapped at the Ridgway terminal. (Guy Dunscomb Coll.) Several years later, at Durango (center), it had lost its distinctive Pierce-Arrow headlights and fenders and acquired a new one-piece windshield glass. (Lad Arend Collection.) No. 7 was graced with an interesting style of lettering in 1939, when it was perched in the yards at Durango. The San Juan has arrived and the Goose will soon depart. (R. H. Kindig.)

The Galloping Goose Reduced to Bare Statistics

	1	2	3	4	5	6	7	SCRR 1
Year Built	6/ /31	8/12/31	12/2/31	5/4/32	6/8/33	1/13/34	10/27/36	Rblt. RGS 11/15/34
Orig. Engine Type	Buick 6 cyl.	Buick 6 cyl.	Pierce-Arrow "33" 6 cyl.	Pierce-Arrow "33" 6 cyl.	Pierce-Arrow "36" 6 cyl.	Buick 6 cyl.	1936 Ford V-8	Pierce-Arrow "80" 6 cyl.
Orig. Engine No.	- - -	- - -	340-796	339-439	- - -	2178774	- - -	809-481
Rblt. Engine Type	- - -	Buick 6	GMC Truck	GMC Truck	GMC Truck	Pierce 6	- - -	- - -
Orig. Body	Buick	Buick 4-door	Pierce-Arrow 1926 "33"	Pierce-Arrow 1926 "33"	Pierce-Arrow 1928 "36"	Buick	Pierce-Arrow 1926 "33"	Pierce-Arrow "80"
Rblt. Body	- - -	Pierce-Arrow "80"	Wayne Bus	Wayne Bus	Wayne Bus	Pierce-Arrow	- - -	- - -
Overall Length	ap. 20′	29′ 11″	43′ 3″	43′ 3″	43′ 3″	25′ 8″	46′	43′ 9″
Length Pilot to Express Body	ap. 14′*	14′ 5″	19′ 3″#	19′ 3″#	19′ 3″#	13′ 8″	20′	19′ 9″
Length Exp. Body	6′ 9″*	16′	24′	24′	24′	12′	26′	24′
width	- - -	7′	7′ 6″	7′ 6″	7′ 6″	7′ 1″	7′ 6″	7′ 6″
height (rail)	- - -	9′ 4″	9′ 8″	9′ 8″	9′ 8″	flatbed	9′ 8″	9′ 8″
Total Weight	5,300 lb.	10,300 lb.	14,800 lb.	14,950 lb.	14,770 lb.	8,700 lb.	16,500 lb.	14,510 lb.
Cost New	$852.58	$1,751.38	$2,586.18	$2,584.56	- - -	- - -	- - -	- - -
Disposition	Scrapped 1933	Colorado Railroad Museum	Knott's Berry Farm	Telluride	Dolores	Brinkerhoff	Brinkerhoff	- - -

* Length after rebuilding to larger passenger capacity.
# Length increased 12″ to accommodate bus bodies.

verbal handle. "Motor", though common on other roads, was too close to motor car to permit unerring identification, and was not really an adequate description of the RGS's trundling trash heap. The latter might have been said for "bus", an unofficial term used more frequently by the RGS in later years. "Bus" calls forth associations of sleekness, speed, comfort, smell, noise, dirt—about half of which applied to the Goose. Somehow, the term "Galloping Goose", while it creates no solid mental image the first time it is heard, is likely better and more appropriate that way. The term is sufficiently odd that it is probably the most effective in dealing with the creation.

Where did the name come from? Some said it was the unmusical sound of the air horn: others said it was because of their waddling gait. Cornelius Hauck credits its invention to an "old-time railroad man" whose jaundiced evaluation was that "darned rig looks like an old goose a-flappin' and a-gallopin' down the track." Josie Crum claimed the term was invented on the spot by the imaginative Mrs. Schools, because it looked to her like a Galloping Goose. Goose? It looked like no goose ever found in the pages of a Zoology book. Perhaps the name resulted from some visual distortion caused by the old home remedies for warding off the winter chill. But given both the ingenuity demonstrated in the construction of these machines and in their naming, it is obvious that originality is not to be counted among absent traits of western-slopers. How the name was ever settled upon and who started it cannot be determined at this writing. It is obvious that the fanciful name was not unique to the RGS. Many railroad operators of gas-electrics referred to their machines as "Galloping Goose". Certainly by the time of the second world war, gas-electrics on the latticework of Northern Pacific branch lines were called by that name. However, despite its application elsewhere, the road known as the "Galloping Goose Route" was the RGS. The name eventually caught on to such an extent that the final evaporation of the road's fortunes found the moniker in use by the RGS itself.

★ ★ ★

In early 1934, the RGS learned that Pierce-Arrow was discontinuing all of the parts for the older models, such as those used on 3, 4, 5 and eventually 7. Odenbaugh claimed that there was no need to buy up a stock of parts. He said that when necessity called, they could buy an engine or a car and have all the parts that they needed.

As originally built, the motors were painted a dark color (possibly coach green), and lettered in a flashy style; the "fast freight" showing that Miller was at least serious about business. No doubt some of the local wits were prone to compare that bold pronouncement with performance, a comparison which would undoubtedly call for a redefinition of the word "fast". It is interesting to note that repainting saw "fast freight" disappear from the RGS, though it must be admitted in all fairness that the inability of the RGS to produce a perfect on-time record was due to the fractiousness of the country as much as the Geese.

In September, 1931, the Southern considered a plan to heat the mail compartment with hot water coursing through pipes running from the engine. However, they were dissuaded by Jack Odenbaugh who claimed that the engines didn't generate enough heat and the system would work only when it was not very cold. Accordingly, they decided to install stoves. Smokebox mesh was later fitted around the stoves, but only after packages were scorched, and the Post Office Department complained that the rope had been burned off one mailbag and the entire top off of another. In the meantime, motormen's nostrils had become playgrounds for a blend of well-nigh overpowering smells—hot engine oil, hot brake shoes, hot radiator water—topped off with hot packages of meat and slightly overdone Sears catalogs.

★ ★ ★

On the RGS, difficulties of a variety of types abounded. There were problems with the D&RGW, problems with terrain and track, problems with motive power, employees and the public. Every now and again, these problems would all come together, and a fast and furious few days would pass before things were back to normal.

There were constant problems with the D&RGW, which had a tendency to charge the RGS excessively for any work done, and seemed to revel in causing problems for their 162 mile neighbor. The Grande also sometimes forgot to tell the RGS what to expect in the way of traffic, and one such incident generated a letter from G. J. Guyer. He complained that the "RGW" had failed to inform the RGS that 21 CCC men and 4 passengers were at Mancos. Departure was delayed for 50 minutes while the load was transferred to number 6, and temporary seats were fixed in the express compartment of number 4. The scenic beauties of the San Juan region were not best admired from the swaying and jouncing express compartment of number 4 in December of 1937.

There was a never-ending stream of reports of rocks on the tracks, soft roadbed, washouts, washins, snow, sagging bridges, and even missing track. Sometimes the intrepid engineers managed to grind to a halt in the nick of time, but not

Carl Fallberg's entertaining Galloping Goose cartoons first appeared in RAILROAD Magazine, and are reprinted here through the courtesy of the artist and RAILROAD.

AFTER LEAVING THE PASTORAL VALLEY OF THE DOLORES RIVER AT RICO, THE TERRAIN BECOMES INCREASINGLY STEEP AND RUGGED, CLIMAXING WITH THE DRAMATIC LONELINESS OF 10,000-FOOT LIZARD HEAD PASS.
No.5
No.5
5
THE HIGH TRESTLES OF THE OPHIR LOOP FOR SOME REASON REMINDED THE DRIVER OF DERAILMENTS HE HAD KNOWN--- INCLUDING THE MEMORABLE MOMENT THEY HOPPED THE TRACK AND WOUND UP 'RIGHT BY THAT POLE THERE!"
5
ALTHO MISHAPS OF THIS SORT ARE RARE — A WHEEL OFF THE TRACK NEAR DOLORES LAID UP No.5 FOR THE NIGHT--- OLD No.7 RESPONDED TO THE EMERGENCY, AND THE BALANCE OF THE TRIP WAS MADE IN REVERSE, AT A BRISK 6 M.P.H.
RIO GRANDE SOUTHERN
No.7
Carl Fallberg '47

always. On February 24, 1938, the number 2 was out of service due to stripped gears or torn-up clutch which was "... caused by motorman Gibbs shifting from high to second he says to avoid striking rock." He was charged with carelessness after having struck a rock on two different occasions, and there was some discussion of giving him a chance to herd sheep rather than Geese.

All of the Geese suffered the indignities of assault by obstreperous rocks and other unforseen difficulties. On the same day in 1935, both numbers 3 and 5 were derailed, the 5 by a plate which came loose and dropped on the track in front of the front truck and number 3 by too much snow on the track. A little later that year, the 3 struck a rock, which necessitated replacement of the crank case, bell housing and one leaf in a front spring. There were probably times when the mechanical department wished they had purchased that stock of Pierce-Arrow parts when they had had the chance.

The weather was a contributing factor in many mishaps—some serious, some not so serious. Just west of the yard limit at Placerville, motorman Laube with number 2 struck an animal. Neither he nor the four passengers saw anything as it was "... storming bad ...". They all felt the impact, and Laube went back to investigate, finding nothing but some red hair on the plow. He surmised that it had been a cow. In this case, there was no damage to report, but in other cases there was.

Goose problems were to an extent the problems of any RGS motive power. Operation over the precipitous terrain, laced together with undulating, contorted trackwork on which maintenance was often of the lick-and-a-promise variety was hard on all mechanical contrivances. Things got so bad that a snowplow derailed not only on the Rico wye (February 19, 1936) but even in the roundhouse. Although Odenbaugh repeatedly demonstrated his expertise at clever Goose construction and maintenance procedures, better results could have been obtained in many cases had he had more money to spend. Thus, it was a constant battle against much bailing wire maintenance for the mechanical birds, and the awesome forces of nature.

Superintendent R. R. Boucher complained in December of 1942 that, "Motor six heats terrible, in fact runs hot going down hill. (That's one for Ripley) ..." but he also offered a solution. "There is a 1930 Buick radiator in Durango which we can buy for $10.00 ..." Perhaps that message signaled the necessity of replacing the Buick machinery with Pierce-Arrow. Like so many RGS puzzles, alterations to the 6 have been obscured by the spoor of the passing years. Pictures taken in 1941 show what appears to be a Pierce-Arrow body on number 6, but this would seem to conflict with this 1942 talk of Buick radiators. Was the body replaced before the engine? What ever the problem was, Jack Odenbaugh managed to rectify it, as he did so many times before and after.

The stove in the Telluride "Motor Car Garage" just couldn't keep the frigid outside outside. It crept in under the doors and around the windows. It was giving the Geese goose-flesh. In the interest of reducing engine wear, the drivers were advised to idle the engines of their Geese for 15 minutes before they left the Telluride aviary.

They also found that they were spending too much money, and were burning the valves of the Goose engines, by buying leaded gasoline (Bronze gasoline). Every year or so, the Continental Oil Company would send the road a summary of the locations at which gasoline was available, and its price. When number 1 was completed, the price ran between 19 and 21 cents per gallon, depending upon location. But by April of 1934, it had rocketed up to between 21 and 23 cents. White claimed that this expensive bronze gasoline had burned valves, and that they had to be replaced. He suggested that a change to white gas (no nepotism involved here) would enable them to avoid problems like that in the future.

Added to these mechanical problems were those of the continual badgering by the Post Office Department, and by the ICC to add this or that, or to make modifications on the Geese. No inconsiderable source of problems were the inexperienced or careless motorman. For example, on February 2, 1933, White wrote a blistering letter to John Crum, accusing him of slipping the clutch on number 2, and calling for assistance when there was nothing actually wrong. He says that his carelessness led to having two steam engines called (at a cost of $60.00) to pull him out. Worse yet, he had broken keys off in two locks, which cost $1.50 each to replace.

★ ★ ★

The fame of the RGS and their Galloping Goose was beginning to spread across the country. The February 1933 issue of the *Express Messenger* Magazine called attention to this "Automobile Train", and praised its performance, saying that it could, "... make 40 to 45 MPH, go up a 4 per cent grade without trouble and buck snowdrifts 2 or 3 feet high with ease." This optimistic report failed to agree with actual operation. For example, March 5, 1933 saw number 2 derailed ½ mile west of MP 55. The front truck derailed on snow drifted into a small cut. Although there was no damage,

Want to build a Goose?

Start with a 1926 Pierce-Arrow model 33 limousine and remove everything between the walls from the windshield to the trunk. Throw the trunk away. Then spread the side walls apart, until there is nearly six feet of air between them at the rear. Build a new rear wall, roof and floor. Add rack and gasoline tanks to the rear portion of the roof. This will give you a very obese Pierce-Arrow—one which is in need of a very carefully prescribed diet. Extend and modify the frame at front and rear. The front will have to be altered to accept a lead truck with 18″ wheels and a spindly pilot: in the case of the RGS, a sheep-catcher. The rear will have to be modified to allow a 24″ wheeled truck to be placed under it so that the cut-down Ford model AA truck differential on the forward axle will connect to the Pierce driveline. Add sprockets to the ends of the axles to accommodate a #100 Whitney chain on each side to drive the rear wheels.

Then frame up an express body of 2″ x 2″ wooden pieces, about 7′ wide, 7′ high and 24′ long. Place this body on a channel steel frame, slip a trailer truck under it, drop the front end over the center truck, garnish with ". . . miscellaneous second hand material from junkyards", and add brakes. Nail steel sheets over the wooden frame, solder together and paint with #2304 Duco primer and coach green paint, or if you prefer the later color, silver. Add lettering, gasoline, radiator water, a few scattered passengers, a bit of mail and express, many dents, and you're in business.

(Plans by John Maxwell)

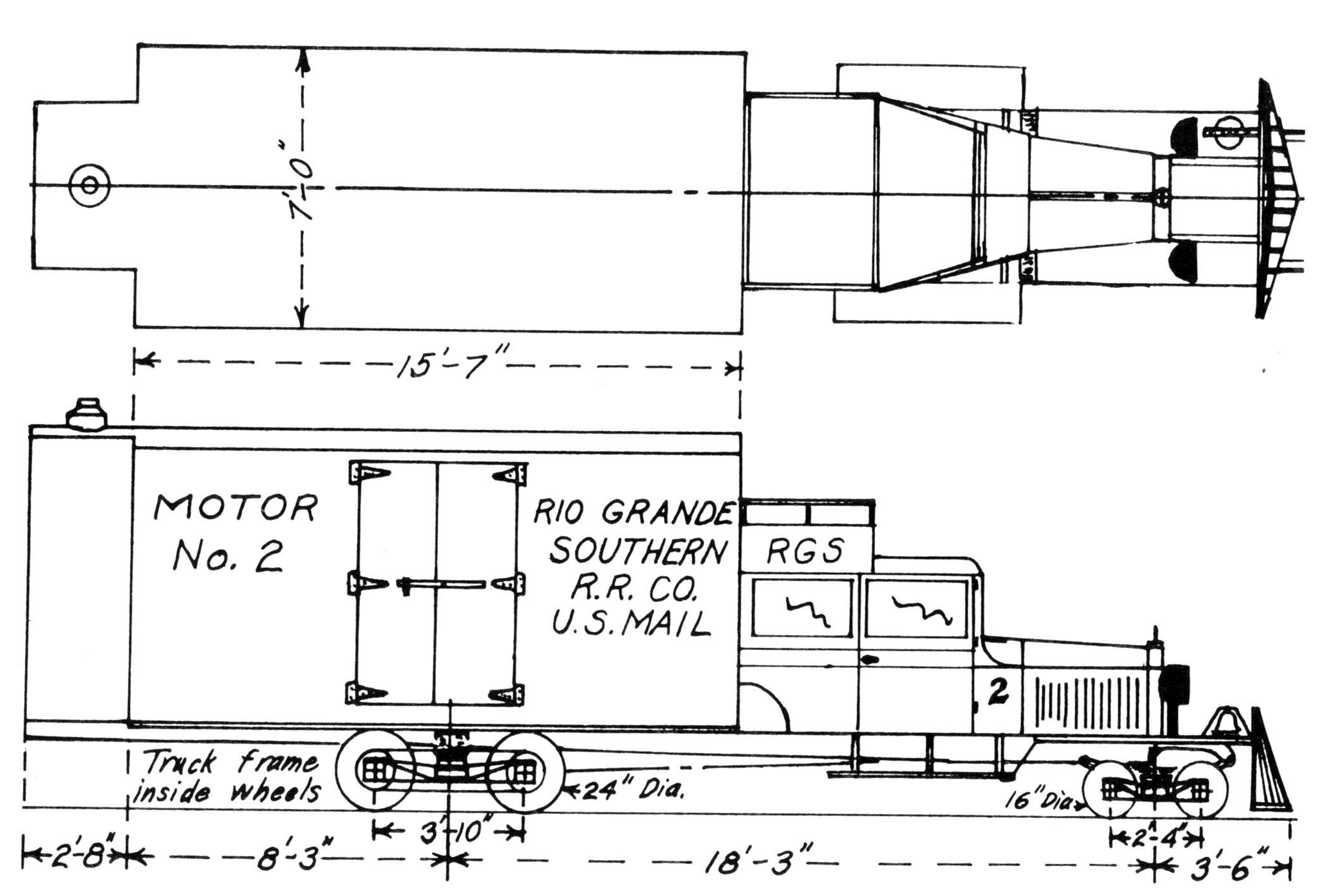

RIO GRANDE SOUTHERN
No 3

RGSo
RIO GRANDE SOUTHERN
No 3

One crisp October morning in 1945 found Bob Richardson journeying north from Dolores on Goose No. 3. While the Goose was loading at Rico, Bob made the panoramic photo at left, with the early morning sun streaming across the wooded hillsides and outlining the stark mine buildings of a departed era. Another stop was made later below Vance Junction (lower left) to transfer passengers, mail and freight for Telluride. On the following day Bob again rode No. 3 southbound, and ran into the sort of contretemps *for which the Geese were noted—it was necessary to unload and wield shovels near Placerville, where a recent shower had brought a mud slide down across the track. The RGS was a line of contrasts, however, and by the time No. 3 reached Trout Lake (below) they were in fresh snow. (All photos, R. W. Richardson.)*

The solitude of the San Juans is reflected in this 1947 vignette at Ophir, one-time booming mining community. The motorman has gone into the depot to discuss world affairs with the agent, and the youthful driver of the kiddie car parked by trackside has followed the excitement indoors. Depot bench and "platform" are bathed in warm mountain sunshine as the lone passenger—one of those "railfan nuts with a camera"—records the scene on film. (C. W. Hauck)

a 4½ hour delay resulted. February 2, 1936, number 2 derailed on ice and snow-packed curve at MP 135.5. Again no damage, but a 5 hour, 10 minute delay. On the same day, interestingly enough, number 2 was involved in another accident . . . this one at Vance Junction. Backing around a curve to the station, the motorman became aware of a plow-flanger standing 25 feet away. The brakes did not hold and the 10,000 pound Goose snuggled up to the 40,000 pound plow-flanger, at a reported speed of 2-3 miles per hour, producing only minor damage.

Enthused by the favorable reports on the Geese in the *Express Messenger* Magazine, the *Christian Science Monitor* and elsewhere, many companies were moved to correspond. On September 9, 1932, a Lincoln dealer in Pasadena, California thought he might be of some assistance to the road. He offered to sell the RGS a fine used 1925 Lincoln sedan for a mere $250.00. The letter appears not to have been answered. A couple of letters were exchanged between the Southern and the Bessemer and Lake Erie, who wrote in early 1933 that they had a 10 mile branch on which there was almost no freight business during the winter, and needed something ". . . cheap and quick . . ." to haul 10 or 12 passengers. The Southern responded by describing the Geese, and concluded that the Goose probably would not fly on the B&LE because of its limited passenger capacity. On March 3, 1933, White replied to a letter from the Shreveport, Houston and Gulf. He described the Geese (it was getting to be a habit) and invited a representative to visit Ridgway.

Not only did the RGS give aid and comfort to other companies suffering from financial drought, and offer to host their master mechanics, they also investigated other roads. For example, Odenbaugh was to leave Ridgway for Denver on April 3, 1933, to look for supplies for a new bus. That would be number 5 which was completed in June. He was to stop on the way to inspect the new Midland Terminal "bus". It would appear that the generic "bus" had in this case been over-extended since the "bus" that Jack Odenbaugh was to look at had been remodeled from a streetcar.

On April 1, 1933, White wrote to Krauser that he would like to hire Lee Elwell to work half time on the new bus, number 5, that Odenbaugh was to be buying parts for. He said that Elwell had been ". . . hanging around here with the idea that Mr. Miller would get the South Park and would get a steady job." Well, the RGS got number 5, but Miller did not get the South Park Branch of the C & S. Had he succeeded in doing so, Elwell might well have had a steady job (he eventually became RGS Master Mechanic) and one might still be riding Galloping Geese down along the South Platte.

★ ★ ★

Although many of the mishaps summarized earlier affected number 2, it was not the only Goose to be involved in accidents and difficulties. But its problems seemed to be so frequent that the RGS had begun talking of unloading it on whomever they could. M. B. Burke of the San Christobal Railroad (the former Lake City Branch of the D & RGW) had, like so many others, been impressed with the success of the large Geese on the Southern. In the spring of 1934, he requested the RGS to rebuild his number 1 along the same lines as RGS number 5. White said that the car would have to be entirely rebuilt. Although the passenger compartment would merely have to be reinforced, ". . . the back baggage compartment will have to be cut off . . . If he just wanted a rear truck put under it without the freight compartment, it could probably be done for about $800.00, but that would leave the body just the same as at present and would not handle any more load than at present time, but would make it operative."

White thought that it would be best to sell number 2 to Burke for $2,000.00. That way the RGS would have some cash, and it would also be rid of number 2. Later on, a price of $1,500.00 was suggested, but number 2 remained on the property. As received from the SCRR, number 1 may have been a Pierce-Arrow with a swiveling front truck and a small baggage compartment tacked on the very back. It might have thus been quite similar to numbers 1 and 2 in many respects, but with a much smaller baggage compartment than number 2.

The rebuilding was completed on November 15, 1934. The machine thus modified was of the same general dimensions and appearance as RGS's highly extolled numbers 3, 4, and 5. It, too, utilized a Pierce-Arrow body as the passenger compartment, but apparently the smaller model "80" two-door style rather than large model "33" four-door. Poor quality pictures show what seems to be an additional section appended to the rear of the Pierce-Arrow body ahead of the express body, resulting in a passenger compartment similar to the RGS geese, but with an overall length six inches greater. The third window (in the added section) appeared to be about half the width of the others. The single headlight was perched atop an "A"-shaped stand in front of the radiator. Aside from these points of difference, rebuilt San Christobal Railroad number 1 was a virtual twin of the RGS numbers 3, 4, and 5.

Four months passed. On March 13, 1935, Krauser took pen in hand and reminded Burke that the job had been finished and that there was the little matter of $837.87 still owed on it. The road had charged 10% for "supervision" for the $2,000 plus job, and still had about $600 of their own money tied up in it. As of June 24, 1935, the "Lake City car" was still on the property, and the RGS was beginning to sound nervous. They were still making out the required monthly reports on it in the hopes that Burke would soon go to his mailbox, find their anxious letters, and show up at Ridgway for his bus. Burke eventually claimed his machine and operated it for a time. The story is incompletely known now, but as more information becomes available, it will be recounted in a future issue of the ANNUAL.

★ ★ ★

Many a San Juan visitor was impressed by the way in which the Geese mastered the difficult terrain. But the Geese did seem to be better at going than at stopping. Braking was chancy at best. The driver was faced with the difficult task of halting a three-truck Goose, weighing almost 15,000 pounds (light), with a combination of front truck brakes actuated by the brake pedal and rear truck brakes actuated by the hand brake lever . . . and sometimes on steep grades. There must have been a good deal of backing up to the depot until the motormen became familiar with the need to decide to stop long before they had to. This leisurely deceleration also bothered the ICC inspector, who was always a little shocked around the RGS. He informed the road that air brakes would be required. On June 30, 1933, a worried Krauser wrote to White that the estimate of $400.00 per car was more than the RGS could rake into one spot. He said, "the cost given by the Westinghouse man is prohibitive, and I think possibly you could work out a cheaper method by applying some of the present train appliances."

Standard brake appliances would be out of the question for a Goose, though. Even a standard one-lung locomotive air pump (if some means could be found to power it) would eat up a large fraction of the payload. A Goose, in its fragility and delicacy, would have shattered if subjected to the pounding and smashing that any piece of normal railroad hardware would be expected to receive in ordinary service. A Goose, ready to leap into motion from the Ridgway station, gas tanks and radiator full, and with a capacity load of passengers would still weigh less than an empty narrow gauge flatcar. Obviously, something of about the weight and cost of bird seed would have been just about right for the air brake system.

There was a long series of letters regarding the installation of air brakes on the Geese. A letter from Superintendent White on July 3, 1933, again notes the ICC requirement to place power brakes on the motor cars. At that time, number 3 was in the shop, and he said that when number 2 had been in for three or four days, Jack Odenbaugh would go to Denver to get material for power brakes. If Odenbaugh made the trip, the files do not show it, and no correspondence developed. By this time, number 5 was in operation, and aside from ironing out a few bugs, there should have been a Goose in almost every depot (which is far classier than merely having a chicken in every pot) up and down to line.

Since Goose number 1 had been retired in 1933, there were just enough passenger Geese to cover all assignments. If the line were severed by high snow or water, or if mechanical trouble kept a Goose out of service, steam would have to be called to fill in. Until operation was cut back by the cancellation of the Dolores-Durango Goose, a normal day's operation took shape thusly: One Goose operated Ridgway-Telluride, a second Telluride-Durango, a third Durango-Dolores, and a fourth Dolores-Ridgway. A diagram of the operation would look something like this:

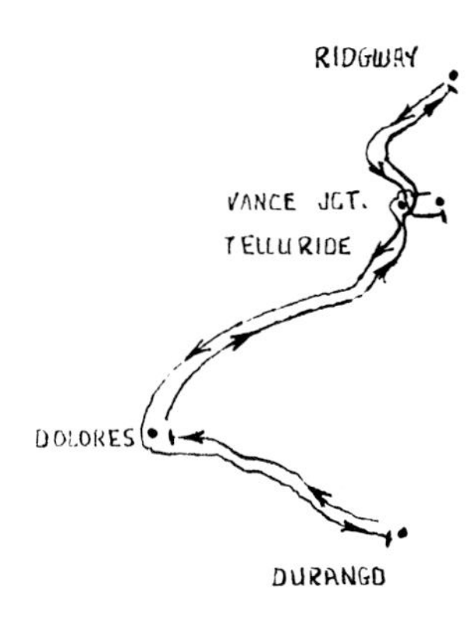

The schedules varied somewhat, but the Goose from Telluride would depart so as to connect with Ridgway Goose at Vance Junction. This allowed a southbound trip (timetable direction, west) to be made in one day. The northbound trip (timetable direction, east), however, required two days.

The eastbound Goose from Dolores (running west, according to the timetable) arrived in Durango to deposit its passengers and express in Durango for shipment east on the next day's D&RGW *San Juan*. The Goose left running west from Durango (or east, according to the timetable) in the evening, after transfer of passengers and express from the arriving *San Juan*. It tied up at Dolores for the night. The next morning, the same Goose left for Ridgway, picking up passengers at Vance Junction who had been patiently waiting there from Telluride to go north (eastward) to Ridgway. In this manner, each Goose would be back in Ridgway every fourth day for inspection and maintenance. If a day were to be allowed for completion of the necessary work, five Geese

By the time (1947) the photograph at right was taken, at the Telluride transfer point, No. 4 and two sister Geese (Nos. 3 and 5) had been rebuilt with Wayne bus bodies and GMC truck engines. Lettering on the box had been modified from the flamboyant herald to a neat serif-face lettering style. Although Grandmother and her shy young granddaughter had undoubtedly appreciated the commodious comfort of the new passenger accommodations, the fact remained that the Goose still galloped primarily for the benefit of the contents of the mail and freight box behind. (C. W. Hauck.) Below, the same No. 4 stops at Peak on a lovely September day to unload the persons and effects of a local indian family, displaying one of the several different convenient avenues of access to the interior of the freight box. The participants show less than no interest in the 455, assisted by a mid-train helper, as it slips past them with a long string of stock cars destined for the high country. (R. W. Richardson)

Bob Richardson was on hand for this triple meet between steam and Geese on Dallas Divide in 1946. Mudhen No. 464, running light, waits while "modernized" Goose No. 3 trundles by, followed by work Goose No. 6. After No. 3's passing, the motorman on No. 6 stops to exchange comments with the 464's engineer before continuing on his way. (Both, R. W. Richardson). The details of No. 6's construction can be seen in the view at bottom, taken during a moment of repose at the Ridgway terminal in 1947. (R. H. Kindig)

September stock rush was often a time in post-war years when it was possible to find the RGS populated both by Geese and steam. On September 15, 1948, Bob Richardson had this good fortune twice in the day. That morning (below), while Goose No. 4 was loading at the Rico depot, far down the main track in the photo, No. 462 was busy assembling a stock extra. In the afternoon, returning on Goose No. 3, he found No. 464 (another of the leased D&RGW Class K-27 2-8-2's the RGS used so extensively in later years) pottering around the depot at Placerville. (Both, R. W. Richardson.)

Lizard Head a half century later: in the early days of the Rio Grande Southern, 2-8-0 No. 12 stopped with a three-car passenger train to show the tourists the wonder of Lizard Head Peak, in the background, and everyone posed for the picture. (Lad Arend Coll.) In 1946, a Rocky Mountain Railroad Club excursion, with Goose No. 4, stopped in a nearly identical location to view this odd rock formation. (R. H. Kindig) In either era, scenery was an attraction for the RGS—and a curse for the operating department.

On the wintry April day in 1908 when RGS 15 stopped at Ophir with the daily passenger train, the town and the railroad both presented pictures of industry and activity. (Lad Arend Coll.) By 1940, when Gerry Best made the photo of the identical location below, steam had given way to Galloping Goose No. 3. The crowd on the platform had dwindled to one Collie dog, and a couple of men disconsolately shovel ore from a pick-up truck into a box car to provide the only sign of economic activity. (G M. Best)

Success of the Galloping Geese meant few instances of steam operation in connection with passenger service. One exception was the occasion at left, caught on film by Bob Richardson, when the 20 and a caboose broke trail through the snow for a Goose, just visible down the track. (R. W. Richardson) Even rarer were steam-powered excursions such as the one below, at Ophir in 1947, headed by RGS No. 455. (Guy Dunscomb Coll.)

would be required to maintain a smoothly functioning system. With only four, overnight maintenance would be required. Apparently cramped by this tight scheduling of maintenance, the RGS determined to add another unit, the 7, to deal with emergencies and to enable them to add a second section now and again. Slightly more than a year after the incident recounted below, at the end of October, 1936, the 7 was pushed out of the nest.

As long as the full operation was continued, the 2, 3, 4, 5 and 7 were busy rocking back and forth from Ridgway to Durango. With the substitution of trucks for the Durango-Dolores and Telluride portions, operation became simpler. Morning departure from Ridgway to Dolores, and an afternoon arrival at the opposite end made only three Geese necessary. In celebration of this "improvement," the RGS happily turned off the key in number 2, and let it sit quietly unless disaster impended. But in the "old days" when only four Geese existed, a major problem would strain the system to its utmost.

Such things happened occasionally. One of the more interesting of these took place beginning on July 2, 1935. Number 2, with motorman Mille, had departed Durango at 5:10 pm with 8,000 pounds of freight and 4 passengers. Everything went well until the drive shaft broke just outside of Mancos. Mille hiked back to a phone, and called the dispatcher. Number 3 had arrived in Durango from Dolores at 5:08 pm, and would normally lay over there until the next evening when it would follow the tracks of the 2 to Dolores. But with the 2 immobilized, the 3 was called to the rescue, and departed Durango, white flags flying, at 8:45 pm. It was coupled to the 2 with its tow bar and after much noise and straining, arrived in Dolores about 3 hours late, at 12:15 am July 3rd. In the meantime, the 6 was sent down from the north, leaving Ridgway at 2:00 am that morning, and arriving at Rico 5:35 am. Later that morning, at 6:15 am, the 3 left Dolores with 2,000 pounds of freight, 1 passenger (the others had mysteriously disappeared before arrival in Dolores) and 7 deadheads, with the 2 in tow. They left Rico at 8:53 am, the 3 still with the 2 in tow, but now with the 6 helping. This triple-headed Goose train ground up to Lizard Head, down into the valley of the sparkling San Miguel, over Dallas Divide and finally eased into Ridgway at 1:40 pm that afternoon, with the 2,000 pounds of freight and one bemused passenger aboard.

Now things were really in a mess. There were at least 2 passenger Geese and the work Goose in Ridgway, with the regularly scheduled Goose due to arrive before long. To relieve this situation, the 6 left for Rico at 2:35 pm, and arrived there at 6:30 pm to continue the interrupted track maintenance work. The 2 was quickly repaired, and sent south (west, that is) again, leaving Ridgway at 11:00 pm, and arriving at Dolores at 4:50 am the morning of July 4th. The 3 had, in the meantime, been sent to Telluride. That would allow the sun to shed its early morning rays on normalcy, as there was then a Goose sitting at each of the required places—Ridgway, Telluride, Dolores and Durango, ready for the day's run. The situation is most intriguing, and an evening's recreation can easily be built around a piece of cardboard, and 5 dice, moving them in the scheduled manner until an interruption such as this occurs. The situation can also be complicated by the insertion of a steam run or two. The RGS lived with this kind of schedule disruption: and though normal trouble-free operation was always striven for, the white flags were always kept within easy reach.

Steam was normally restricted to heavy freight but could be called out to extricate a Goose from its snowy nest. On March 3, 1935, number 2 left Telluride at 8:35, Vance Junction at 10:35 (normally a 30 minute run), and struggled into Mancos at 3:10 pm. It was followed all the way by the 6 which had come along to render assistance and to pick up the pieces. The battle with the elements continued, and finally halted the caravan at milepost 143. Superintendent White left the entourage, and tramped through snow on foot for 2 miles into Hesperus to summon help. Engine 42 responded from Durango, and hauled the two snow-stranded birds to the shelter of Durango's warm roundhouse.

The recipe on the RGS seems to have been, "immerse a Goose in hot water, and create a stew." An example was revealed by R. W. Richardson, who in reading train sheets of the RGS (temporarily misplaced in the labyrinth of the Colorado Railroad Museum), came upon the following incident. Leaving the Lizard Head section house, a Goose and its occupants were thrown into one such stew. As the Goose burst from the lower end of the snowshed, the driveshaft snapped and flailed around with such abandon that it severed the air line. The accelerating Goose would not obey the now-lifeless air brake valve. The motorman and passengers implored it to stop, but to no avail. Egged on by the combined forces of a recalcitrant mechanical increpitude and some 3% of gravity, the Goose surged down toward Trout Lake.

Its fleet-flanged progress momentarily damped by the relatively level circuit of the lake, the Goose's captives prepared to leave its comfort and fend for themselves until things quieted down a little. They threw open the door, and heaved themselves out into a fortuitously located snowdrift, starting with an infant and ending with the captain of the rapidly sinking ship.

Hotfooting it to a nearby phone, the motorman called Mrs. Belisle, the Postmistress and Station Agent at Ophir, and warned her that his Goose had just flown the coop. In the unlikely event it should remain on the track, he told her, it should be tearing through Ophir forthwith. Mrs. Belisle had nothing handy for halting a loose Goose, but stepped out to see if she might perceive its approach. As she looked, the Goose careened around the curve and out over the high trestle, bent for the bottom of the hill. With a ghostly clatter, neither slowing as required by regulations, nor giving warning other than the flapping of its tin feathers, the pilotless machine galloped around the curves, whooshed past the station and rocketed out onto the long lower trestle. It munched into a snowdrift and almost stopped, but burst through, canted around Butterfly, screeched around Windy Point and was gone.

She quickly called Vance Junction and alerted the section men. Those worthies, to whom calamity and entanglements were routine, stoically picked up a wrecking chain, walked up the track a ways, and threw it across the rails. One of the gang, being a member of the "if one drop of oil is good, two is better" fraternity, threw a second chain across the track a little further down. They retired into the brush to await developments, but did not have long to ponder the possible results of their ministrations. With a muted clickety-clack, the Goose was upon them. Its front wheels hit the first chain, slowed, and then clumped noisily over. The other wheels followed like a flock of sheep, making a horrible din, and thoroughly stirring up the sediment in the gas tanks. But its progress had been sufficiently arrested that upon striking the second chain, the front wheels locked, and the runaway Goose was brought to a sparking, shuddering stop.

Scheduled speed between Lizard Head and Vance Junction was about 24 mph. The erstwhile runaway had made it in far less time than that. It is easy to see that the RGS could have speeded up its operations considerably had they merely decided to eliminate the motormen. Nobody can ever know for sure, but there appears to be good reason to believe that riding a driverless Goose through the sinuousity of Mear's Puzzle and Ophir Loop would have been an exciting experience indeed.

★ ★ ★

In January, 1934, prompted by the urgings of the ICC, the RGS began to look for an anti-goose warning device. An estimate then showed a $1000.00 price tag for an air system, and the company objected to it on the grounds of expense. If one were to count grade crossings and divide into the purchase price, some several years of operation would still render a very high price per honk. But with the ICC breathing down their necks, it was clear that something had to be done, so in January a sample siren (on approval) was ordered for trial on a Goose. There is no record of the outcome of the test. Perhaps someone will come forward to tell about a Goose screaming into Ridgway, and rousing volunteer fire departments from a dozen towns up and down the line . . .

In the continuing effort to improve the Geese (this time not under the prod of the ICC), the RGS on February 24, 1934 inquired about the possibility of using rubber cushioned wheels on the Geese. The company's reply is not to be found in the records. Perhaps the road decided that it would not be worth the expense, or maybe they worried that if the Geese bounced more than they already did, they would become airborne even more frequently.

But the ICC inspector continued finding things for the Southern to add to the Geese. On June 24, 1935 it was sanders for all cars. One would think that the roller coaster profile of a road such as the RGS would make sanders a must. In fact, the filed examples of busses bumping into cars or sailing loftily past the appointed stopping place should have convinced them of the need. Then again, perhaps with hand brakes, the only conditions under which a man could lock the wheels would be on icy track. Certainly from the motorman's viewpoint, depressing the foot brake and pulling on the hand brake at the same time, when added to such things as ringing the bell, putting in the clutch, taking it out of gear, etc., was enough without having to worry about operating the sanders, too.

The ICC must have been getting impatient. Finally on July 29, 1938 (5 years after they had first been advised to apply air brakes), a notarized statement shows air brakes to have been installed on both the 3 and 4, with the 5 following on April 27, 1939. Goose operators by this time might well have been capable of equalling some of the legendary feats of strength of Pecos Bill or Paul Bunyan.

With the adoption of a non-standard straight air system, the Geese could not be cut into a train line, and if a steam engine were to be hauling a Goose, the Goose could derail, and the engineer would never know. With the locomotive banging away at the snow drifts, and snow swirling around into the cab and tender, no one on board the engine could see the Goose even if it were coupled onto the tender with its special drawbar. Such a practice was not unknown as a means of getting the Goose through a drift that it would otherwise have stalled in, and this rather precarious existence for the Goose, flopping along through the snow behind the locomotive, was not known to elicit kind remarks from anybody who experienced it. Had a Goose ever become badly derailed, it would have been dragged squealing and disintegrating until the motorman was left standing on an articulated flatcar, a brake lever grasped firmly in his hand.

A small compressor driven by the engine maintained a main reservoir pressure of 80 pounds, while the cylinders operated on 40 pounds. The nature of the original cylinder installation is not clear, but at the end of operation, the Geese were equipped with the truck-type pot cylinders on each of the two rear trucks. The hand brake arrangement was retained on those trucks, with the result that there were almost as many ways of stopping a Goose as there were of stopping a Manitou and Pikes Peak cog train. In case of emergency, the motorman could always join the birds, and wait for the Goose to do the same. One can conjure up a picture of a Goose flapping down a remote mountainside, leaving shards of metal feathers dangling from rocks and trees, but it never happened. They ran away, they derailed (uncountable times), they were dented by rocks and trucks, they were assaulted by snow, they had bearings burned out, they had transmissions and clutches damaged and still they were patched up and continued running.

Only God and Jack Odenbaugh know what changes were made on the Geese down through the years. There is no known running tally of modifications made and parts replaced, but it is clear that a number of major modifications were made. The paint scheme was changed to silver on the 2, 3, 4, 5 and 6. The express doors were moved up to the center of the express body on 3, 4, and 5. The original Pierce-Arrow frog-eyed fenders were removed from the 3 and 4, but remained on the 5 into World War II. Air brakes and horns were added and new engines were installed. The Pierce-Arrow bodies on 3, 4, 5, were replaced with Wayne bus bodies. Finally, in the last year of operation, the express bodies were modified to carry passengers. There were innumerable replacements of miscellaneous fittings, grindings of crankshafts and valves, rebuildings of transmissions, replacements and substitutions of hardware and equipment, and numerous minor modifications.

The available records fail to show either the reason or the date for modification of the express bodies to place the door in the center. Pictures of the shiny new number 7 show it with the express doors in the center, and painted aluminum. As noted earlier, the original paint was dark, but after an exchange of letters, White on September 25, 1934 said that Odenbaugh seemed to think that it would be a good idea to paint the Geese aluminum. Aluminum paint stands up to the weather very well, and paint jobs could be expected to last quite a number of years. A single coat of paint has lasted for well over 10 years on the 2 at the Museum.

The installation of "new" (perhaps "newer" would be more correct) engines in the Geese has been documented elsewhere. The 2 wore its engine out quite early, and it was presumably replaced in 1935. Even careful, continual maintenance on the big Geese could not stretch the life of their engines much beyond the end of World War II. Estimating about 2,000 miles per month, each of the big Geese would have logged around a quarter of a million miles by the time their engines were replaced with war surplus GMC truck engines in 1946. At that time, the 3, 4, and 5 were also rebuilt with bus bodies replacing the Pierce-Arrow bodies. Number 7 retained its Pierce-Arrow passenger body to the end. While the original bodies had been deemed capable of accommodating 10 passengers (a generous estimate, probably based on the narrowest-beamed member of the shop force), the new design was said to hold 12. It would help if the passengers were all on good terms. To hold the more commodious body, the front frame was lengthened and reinforced.

From time to time, other modifications not reflected in the official records were made. Although it is frequently difficult to imagine what has happened, close inspection of each car will reveal small idiosyncracies. As an example of the way in which changes were made, Goose number 2 at the Colorado Railroad Museum carries the scars of many modifications. Early pictures of this car show it to have been built with a small four-door Buick body. That body was replaced sometime in the 1930s with one from a small Pierce-Arrow (model 80). The new body was longer than the old one. To accommodate it without rebuilding the frame and driveline, the express body was shortened about 8 inches. Where did the new body come from? Pierce-Arrows seemed to be popular in Colorado, and Odenbaugh could probably have acquired a used one quite easily.

But there is a more intriguing possibility. Although the "Lake City car" was apparently used on the former Lake Fork branch of the D&RGW by Burke, its disposition is unknown. It has been suggested that with the abandonment of the operation in 1939, the car came back to the RGS, who used the original Pierce "80" 2-door passenger body, hood and radiator to replace those on the 2. The roof box on which the gas tank rests has been painted since the 1930s, but a part of the San Christobal Railroad name still shows through the paint.

It is a reasonable assumption that the RGS did not replace the bodies on the 2, 3, 4 and 5 for cosmetic reasons. They must have been weak, rotten (the original bodies were framed in wood) or damaged to merit replacement.

★ ★ ★

The post-war tourist rush also affected the RGS. Various fan groups descended upon the Silver San Juan Scenic Route, and galloped up and down the inclines and declines, gasped at the declevities and caused the heirs of George Eastman to wax exceeding glad. Crusty goose-herder Jimmy Cooper claimed that he had worn his (amputated) index finger down to a stub pointing out scenic wonders to enthralled passengers. Those who rode the Goose came home with a hatful of interesting stories, and an impression that the RGS had put more cars on the ground and over the edge of precipices than they had ever managed to keep on the track.

Indeed, it has been the habit of those who have delt with the Southern to concentrate upon the accidents, injuries and deaths which accumulated down through the years. The verticality of the terrain has also been repeatedly emphasized, and given this latter fact, it is remarkable that the railroad was no more effective at filling San Juan graveyards that it was. Goose drivers seemed to delight in pointing out the exact spot where all the trains they could remember (and a few they apparently fabricated) had derailed and gone tumbling down ashpan over steam dome to the very bottom of a fearsome chasm.

With improvement in the nearby highway, shippers began to rely more and more heavily upon highway transport (a euphemism for "truck"). Given the imposition of a surcharge on each car of freight handled on the road, and a reduction in service, shippers began eying the highway. It is true, however, that the RGS itself was instrumental in convincing shippers that the highway was more reliable. In January of 1949 an unusually heavy snow descended softly upon the San Juans, and the Lizard Head portion of the route was blocked. The rotary, on its way to open the line, exploded at Vance Junction. A clamshell crane and bulldozers battled the continuing snow on the pass for ten days, and finally gave up. The new Receiver, J. Pierpont Fuller, Jr., who had been appointed the previous year, suspended operation until the line could be opened in May. Almost as soon as trains were ready to roll, zinc and lead prices tumbled, and the mines closed. An unexpectedly warm June increased snowmelt, and the resulting high water carried away portions of the track and roadbed between Dolores and Ophir. Where bean shipments had been increasing before, they then began to fall to the trucks. The Geese did not operate until August 2nd, and then only Ridgway-Rico. Nevertheless, 14 of the staunchest of railfans made their way to Rico for a ride. Fuller claimed that one more flood like this would finish the RGS.

All of this adversely affected the promptness with which the mail reached its destination. When flood effects were added to such things as Geese on the ground and out of gas (in this latter case, a steam engine sent to rescue the dry Goose was derailed), the residents became progressively more difficult to mollify. "We are always glad to get our mail . . . but when we don't get it, we all go home figuring maybe we'll have better luck next day!" one un-lettered man observed.

The next winter, the road grounded the Geese and handled the mail in company trucks. This cavalier attitude was not appreciated either by the Post Office Department or by the residents. The Post Office was chagrined that it had been paying premium rates to the RGS for quite casual service. They notified Fuller that they would let a new mail contract as of April 1st which would leave the RGS not holding the bag. Business had dropped 40% in 1949 according to General Manager C. W. Graebing, and Fuller foresaw the end. He asked basin residents to write the Post Office Department and their Congressman in the vain hope of restoring the mails to the rails. The loss of the mail contract was the death blow to the RGS, but the carcass continued to kick weakly into the winter of 1951.

On May 12, 1950, Federal Judge Knous gave formal permission to discontinue scheduled runs of the Geese. None had been operated since the previous December 18th. In August of 1950, Bob Richardson estimated that since the regular Dolores Goose had been grounded, Dolores tourist traffic had declined by 50%. But the RGS continued to do the small things that meant so much to their passengers. In the summer of 1950, a construction program produced two small buildings at Trout Lake which must have been a welcome

With loss of the mail contract and suspension of regular scheduled service, management decided to convert exclusively to excursion service. Freight compartments of the four big Geese were converted to passenger use, and advertising signs and other facilities erected. (Top, Trout Lake: R. W. Richardson. Bottom right, Ridgway: Ed Randow, Mike Decker Coll. Bottom left, R. W. Richardson.)

RIO GRANDE
SOUTHERN
4

Tourists quickly followed railfans to ogle at the wonders of the Ophir Loop. Above left, No. 4 negotiates the lower trestles along the cliffs approaching Ophir (Museum Coll.), while at center No. 3 gingerly crosses the long trestle at Ophir (R. W. Richardson). Bottom left, No. 4 scoots over Bilk trestle near Vance Junction, one of innumerable smaller trestles on the RGS (R. H. Kindig). On this page, Bob Richardson has caught the No. 3 working its way past the great cliffs approaching Ophir — a favorite spot for Goose motormen to point out real and imaginary debris from old wrecks, way down in the valley below. (R. W. Richardson) All these photographs were made during the summer of 1951, the second and last year in which the Goose excursion service was offered; that fall, the railroad ground to a final halt.

sight indeed to the weary fans who made it that far. Few people would have the intestinal fortitude to last more than 49 miles in a jouncing, jolting Goose without some kind of relief. To save the saturated passengers from the possibility of a dreadful mistake, the RGS thoughtfully adorned one door with a goose and the other with a gander.

In 1950 the road converted the express bodies to passenger carrying by filling the side doors, cutting a narrow door in the rear, and incising a long open window into each side, almost the entire length of the body. Seats and a "snack bar" were also installed. With these modifications, passenger capacity was increased to 32. However, it is obvious that even four Geese, with a capacity of about 32 persons each, would not serve to put the road back into the black unless they were also to engineer holdups and take not only the passenger's money and watches, but the fillings in their teeth as well.

As the Geese staggered up and down, brimming with enthusiastic camera clickers, the road continued its quest for freight business. On September 22, 1950, the 455, on such an errand, lost its tender, and it rolled down a bank. The crew managed to push it a bit farther down to the road, and the county cat-skinner towed it up to the nearest crossing where the wanderer was reunited with its more orderly companion. Shortly after, the stock season began, and by the time business had slackened enough to release men to operate the Geese, it was too cold for tourist business. Until March of 1951, snow had been light enough for operations to continue, and many cars of ore were hauled from the mines at Rico and Telluride. Infrequent runs had also been made to Dolores and Rico from Durango. Since the Telluride mine had decided to ship its ore by truck beginning on June 1, the only large shipper left was the Rico-Argentine mine at Rico. They were also considering the possibility of shipping their 30 or 40 monthly narrow gauge carloads by truck, a practice they began on October 15.

Goose operation was planned for the period between June 1 and October 1. Every Saturday and Sunday at 9 am, a Goose was scheduled to leave Ridgway for Lizard Head, and another was to operate Durango-Dolores. This run was later changed on Sunday to a Dolores-Lizard Head round trip. The season saw 2,000 passengers handled from Ridgway, an increase of 100% over the previous year. There was a faint hope that the road might somehow be able to continue operation, even with reduced trackage. Yet the RGS appeared to be more valuable dead than alive to some, who thought that there was an opportunity to make it pay off one final time. Many residents hoped that the demise of the railroad would mean better highways, and almost anything would be better than some they had then. With incidents of ore trucks churning up the road and smashing through bridges, it would be some time before that hope would be realized.

Fuller wanted to suspend service as of November 1. There was enough cash on hand to continue operations the following summer, but not through the winter. Local business was down to only a few cars a month, hardly enough to justify keeping the road open. Sale appeared unlikely, as the interested parties were not able to raise the required half million dollars scrap value. Public sentiment appeared to be in favor of allowing the road to continue as long as it could, and seemed to be happy about the tourist business which it had brought to the area. Most of the counties, though eager for back taxes, appeared not to be officially in favor of abandonment. However, as a result of meeting with attorneys representing each of the five counties through which the tracks lay, Receiver Fuller prepared applications for abandonment. Even as Fuller labored to bring operations to a halt, the dauntless little trains continued their struggle against the forces of gravity as they had for almost 60 years. In the middle of November, cars of the D&RGW were beginning to be collected, with final runs anticipated before the end of the month. Problems with snow and cold stalled the official last runs til December.

After final permission to abandon was granted on April 8, 1952, the Hyman-Michaels firm of Chicago acquired the scrap assets for $409,000.00. The sale stipulated that the line was to be scrapped, and that no part of it was to be sold for operation. On September 2, the first rail was lifted from the embrace of its spikes and the dissolution commenced. Even this last act was joined by the Geese, which, in various states of dismemberment, helped to rend rail from tie and thus to wind up the affairs of the road forever.

It has been shown how the operation of number 1 was adjudged to have saved the cost of its construction in a month's time, a truly amazing savings. It may be taken for fact that the origin and evolution of the Goose enabled the RGS to feather its nest for a few more years. In September, 1930, operation with steam had cost $8,294.58, while in September of the following year, a year of partial Goose operation using number 1 and 2, expenses amounted to only $1,807.04; a notable savings. In this figure of differential cost, the secret of the RGS's longevity is exposed. Perhaps without the considerable savings resulting from the use of the

Geese, the RGS might well have folded up its tracks and stolen quietly away before the beginning of World War II. If that had happened, the Manhatten project might not have been the roaring success which it proved to be, and thousands of tourists and railfans would have been the poorer for not having experienced the trestles of Ophir. Yet, had the line continued in business much beyond its expiration, indications are that long-delayed replacement of ties and rails at some locations, and bridge rebuilding would have had to have been undertaken.

The mileage figures also illustrate their dependence upon Geese as the prime movers. In January, 1937, the following figures were run off:

All Goose mileage 10,729.

All steam mileage 8,509 (as 40 and 41 were being shopped, this figure includes only engines 20, 22, 25, 42 and 455).

In the middle of the war, the December, 1942 mileage stood at:

Number 2	162 miles
Number 3	1,134 miles
Number 4	2,016 miles
Number 5	2,382 miles
Number 6	686 miles
Number 7	1,878 miles

For a total of 8,256 Goose miles.

At the same time, steam power consisting of Engines 20, 22, 40, 41, 42, 340*, 455, 462*, and 464* chalked up only 6,072 miles. (*D&RGW engines)

With the loss of both mine business and the mails, the mechanical marvels could not further prolong the life of the RGS, even in the face of such statistics. Otto Mears' Silver San Juan Scenic Route had been in financial trouble almost from the moment it was finished. For a while, it didn't matter. Prior to the advent of dependable highways and dependable highway transportation, it had served a useful, if not always sufficiently remunerative function. But even though the automobile was the ultimate downfall of the RGS, it was also its temporary salvation. The RGS survived in spite of the odds, and it survived because a band of resolute, inventive men thought it was worth while doing. And so they did it, and though the world never really knew or cared, some cheered, and the Geese galloped and man's needs and desires were served and the sun shone on the San Juans.

The sun still shines on the San Juans, but it now shines on rotten ties and eroding grades. Even twenty years after the fact, it was a remarkable railroad in a remarkable place. The Galloping Geese were remarkable machines, and if it weren't for the pictures, some people might be prone to believe that the whole story had been invented by a Western slope wag. The Goose no longer gallops except in the hearts of those who knew it and can imagine it, and there it shall gallop forever.

Acknowledgements

Most of the information came from RGS company files at the Colorado Railroad Museum. Some portions of the information on corporate history are from Josie Moore Crum's *Rio Grande Southern Story* (Railroadiana, Inc., Durango, 1957). Other details are from C. W. Hauck's *The Case of the Disappearing Pierce-Arrows* (Antique Automobile, August-September, 1959) and early issues of the *Narrow Gauge News*, published by Bob Richardson and Carl Helfin at South Alamosa.

Further information on the Model T Ford operated on the C&S came from correspondence with Bruce Triplett. Robert W. Richardson was, as usual, an invaluable source of hints and suggestions. Mr. Richardson and Jim Dunlop listened patiently to the entire first draft, while Gordon Chappell read and critically commented on the manuscript at a late stage of its formulation. Both he and the editor were kind enough to make many valuable suggestions for the improvement of the article, but must be considered blameless. Also innocent of the whole affair was my wife, Kay, to whom fell the horror of producing legible copy, in English, from the bits and pieces of notes. Interpretation of the data is the responsibility of the author, who claims that if there was any humor about this business, it was in the Rio Grande Southern Railroad itself: a streak of rust built too late, too long and too twisty, but too tough to give up.

In later years Geese flew into Telluride only on excursion flights of one sort or another. Nos. 3 and 5 made it in July, 1946 on a Rocky Mountain Railroad Club trip; both are seen at the depot (top) (R. H. Kindig), while No. 5 can be observed below negotiating the wye (Jackson Thode). Five years later the 3 returned on one of the railroad's own excursions (Museum Coll.).

Goose excursion runs were much less frequent on the south end of the line in 1950 and 1951. However, Ernie Peyton was on hand for a run with No. 5 in August, 1951, and snapped this dramatic portrait as it paused at the Mancos depot. The stormy sky was an appropriate background for the Southern at this stage of its life. (Guy Dunscomb Coll.) Below, a year earlier Goose No. 4 was poised at the Durango depot, ready to depart ahead of the D&RGW's San Juan, *in a photo encompassing two of the most lamented of departed modes of transportation: the Galloping Goose and the narrow gauge steam luxury passenger train. (C. W. Hauck)*

The last trips on the Telluride branch were made by No. 3, its body almost entirely cut away, converted to a work Goose for the lugubrious purpose of tearing up the line. Top, Dick Kindig found it near Pandora (end of the branch) on September 15, 1952, and (center) Bob Richardson found it further down the branch on the 25th. No. 4 had been placed on a section of track in Telluride (bottom; R. W. Richardson) as a memento of pleasanter times.

(R. W. Richardson)

Sic Transit Gloria: *It remained for the Galloping Goose, that wonderful creation of desperation that saved the Rio Grande Southern a score of years earlier, to be the instrument of death for the Railroad. October 1952 found the No. 7, its freight box removed and trailing a flat car, tearing up the rails near Montelores. The beautiful fall weather was deceptive; the 7 was presiding at the funeral of its own Railroad. The end had come and there was no going back.*

A Goose Review

Amazingly, six of the seven Geese hatched over half a century earlier are still alive. Goose No. 2, the result of the amalgamation of first No. 2 and the San Cristobal Goose, was little used in later years and sat idle in the Ridgway yards. Bob Richardson rescued it and removed it to Alamosa for preservation. Soon after a cosmetic renovation, Bob took a photo of it posed with John Crum, long-time RGS conductor and motorman, and his wife Josie Moore Crum. In 1958 No. 2 progressed to its present home in Golden, shown in these other photos. Returned to operating condition, No. 2 has proven very popular for occasional demonstration rides for Museum visitors. Even on the rare rainy day at Golden (right), would-be riders line up in anticipation.

R.G.S.
3
3
R.R.CO.
U.S.MAIL

RGS
3
3

RGS
RGS
RIO GRANDE SOUTHERN
No 3
3
3

No. 3 *was the first of the "mainstream" large Geese, and its original form and dress matched that of No. 4 shown on page 10. Otto Perry photographed it on May 27, 1939, at Durango and Franklin Junction in its second decor, and leaving Rico on June 30, 1940, resplendent in new paint and displaying the stylistic new Rio Grande Southern herald. The distinctive Pierce-Arrow headlamp-fenders had disappeared. By September 1948, when Bob Richardson photographed it at the Telluride transfer stop, the Pierce body had also disappeared in favor of the new, more commodious Wayne bus body. Finally, the same Goose appeared at Lizard Head in 1951 in excursion service, with freight body rebuilt to accommodate sightseers (R. W. Richardson photo).*

Rare Snapshot *of a Goose in operation with the original dark color scheme is this early 1930's view at Ophir, probably of the No. 4, showing a neatly attired young woman and boy posed on the running board — evidence that not all passengers were Indians or prospectors. The late 1930's view at Durango shows the 4 with the succeeding paint combination, but still equipped with the traditional Pierce headlamp-fenders (Museum Coll.). By the time Bob Richardson snapped No. 4 at the Telluride transfer in 1945, the fenders were gone and the new RGS herald had been applied. Jack Thode was on a June, 1949 Rocky Mountain Railroad Club excursion powered by ex-Colorado & Southern No. 74, when they came upon No. 4 at Matterhorn. Suffering from some mechanical malady, the 4 had to be shoved into a siding by No. 74 before the excursion could continue. By now a Wayne bus body and conservative lettering had been applied. Finally, Bob Richardson took the posed "portrait" (bottom) on May 23, 1951, when the 4 had been converted to excursion use.*

74
RIO GRANDE
SOUTHERN
No. 4

THE GALLOPING GOOSE
RIO GRANDE
SOUTHERN
4
OPHIR LOOP
LIZARD HEAD
SCENIC LINE
THOMPSON PARK
DOLORES CANON

Flagship *of the Goose fleet when constructed was No. 5. Adapted from a later model (1928) Pierce "36" limousine — then only 5 years old — it must have presented a spiffy appearance when new, as attested by the two views below, made at Dolores and Durango in July 1933 by Donald E. A. Rogers. Opposite: by the time Otto Perry took these photos at Placerville (top) and Dolores in 1940, the former jewel looked distinctly dingy in its revised paint scheme, but was essentially intact as built. Bob Richardson's shot taken at Grady in 1951, when the 5 had been converted to excursion use, clearly shows the dramatic changes that had taken place in the intervening decade.*

RGS
RGS
No 5
5

DOLORES
ELEV. 6957
RGS
RGS
RIO GRANDE SOUTHERN
No 5
5

THE GALLOPING GOOSE
RIO GRANDE SOUTHERN
5
OPHIR LOOP
LIZARD HEAD
SCENIC LINE
THOMPSON PARK
DOLORES CANON

RIO GRANDE SOUTHERN R.R.
R.G.S.
No.
6
KEEP OFF
KEEP OFF

D&RGW
9285
6
6
RGS

Work Goose *No. 6 has survived over a half century of hard labor and abuse quite well, and now enjoys retirement operation at the Colorado Railroad Museum hauling occasional passengers seated on borrowed depot benches. After a good snow, the prospect of such a ride seems less inviting. (Museum photos.) A curious puzzle is presented by a comparison of the 1935 Donald E. A. Rogers photo of No. 6, top left, and Bob Richardson's 1952 view below; the hood and bodywork are clearly different. The 1952 (and present) bodywork is clearly of Pierce "33" origin, but the earlier version is so far a mystery, bearing closest resemblance to the work of custom body-builder Judkins.*

MOTOR
No. 7
RIO GRANDE SOUTHERN
R.R.CO.
R. G. S.
7

RIO GRANDE
SOUTHERN
No. 7
7

Final *Goose venture was No. 7, which appeared from an accumulation of Pierce Model "33" and Ford parts in 1936. Jack Thode found it leaving Durango on June 30, 1939, at 6:16 PM, implying a delay due to a late connection from D&RGW train 115. When Otto Perry snapped it trundling out onto the Ophir trestle in 1940, the new paint scheme was in evidence. After its arrival at the Colorado Railroad Museum it ventured out on Museum trackage in "non-revenue excursion service," but its decrepit condition became all too apparent one day when a breeze blew the body off the chassis, and much-needed rebuilding was promptly scheduled.*

Colorado Rail Annual

A Journal of Railroad History in the Rocky Mountain West

Published by the Colorado Railroad Museum, the *Colorado Rail Annual* provides a format for publication and thereby preservation of knowledge acquired through detailed and serious research into the history of the railroad industry in the Rocky Mountain West, especially the narrow gauge lines in the Colorado Rockies. Articles on such topics incidentally include much local history of towns and industries in the region. The *Colorado Rail Annual* provides a means of distributing and insuring the preservation of significant historical information contained within the manuscript, personal papers and corporate records collections of the Colorado Railroad Museum and other libraries and depositories, all of which help to explain from the point of view of at least one industry how Colorado and the Rocky Mountain Region became what they are today. Through extensive use of illustrations and maps, the *Colorado Rail Annual* serves also to preserve the graphic record of a part of the Rocky Mountain past. Finally, the profits from sale of the publication all go to help the Colorado Railroad Museum to persevere in its mission.

The Colorado Railroad Museum is the property of the Colorado Railroad Historical Foundation, a non-profit educational organization whose objective is to preserve to the limits of its ability tangible documentary, graphic, and artifactual remains of the railroads which have operated in the Rocky Mountain West. This program is centered at the Colorado Railroad Museum in Golden, Colorado, where there is a collection of a number of locomotives, passenger cars, freight cars, work cars, a half mile of track, switch stands, lanterns, tools — indeed all kinds of the physical remains of Rocky Mountain railroading. In a building resembling an old depot, the Museum exhibits photographs, documents, dining car china, ticket punches, and all the smaller categories of artifacts associated with Colorado railroad history. Here, too, the Museum maintains, at present without formal staffing, an excellent library of books, documents and archives pertaining to railroad history, including document collections representing segments of the official records of many Colorado railroads. On occasion the Museum operates some of its rolling stock, its locomotives and cars, thus recreating if only momentarily a glimpse of the past, a sort of "living history."